ABC'S of LEADERSHIP

Uncommon Leaders from the Bottom Up

By
Effua McGowan

ABC's of Leadership

Uncommon Leaders from the Bottom Up

Copyright 2020 by Effua McGowan

All Rights Reserved

**A GIFT FROM ME TO YOU JUST TO
SAY THANK YOU!**

Leadership Guide

R. E. L. A. Y.

Ready

Encourage

Leader

Anchor

You

TO DOWNLOAD, GO TO:
https://www.subscribepage.com/t5s5a2

Dedication

For my mother Cecelia who believed in my endless possibilities. And my Papie Tom from whom I heard the essence of courage and boldness in driving your purpose. May they continue to smile proudly at me from among the Saints.

INTRODUCTION

When you think about a leader, you often think of someone who is in a higher position than where you sit in the chain of command: but that is the furthest from the truth. A leader is someone who influences change, no matter how small. Who creates an environment where others can realize their potential? A leader is one who unconsciously gives others permission to dare to be "all they can be." A leader unleashes the potential of others effortlessly. A leader is one who is motivated by growth all around. A leader may or may not lead a team. An uncommon leader strives for superior self-management which translates to a shift in paradigm. An uncommon leader is relatable, authentic and to some extent, mysterious. Ever present, yet ever evolving.

In some instances, leadership may mimic parenthood. A role that fuses both guiding and caring for others. So, this book is really about the traits that leaders have and how you can adopt or reinforce in self and others. These behaviors are timeless and evolutionary in simple yet profound ways. These traits are hopefully, the ones that you aspire to embrace.

It is our desire that you identify opportunities to recognize and apply these traits, thereby creating your own blueprint. We invite you to make the paradigm shift and embrace them and make them your own. In doing so, you activate the leader that is not like everybody else, but the uncommon leader that stands out and makes a real difference, for self and others.

I mean who do you want to be? A commoner or the uncommoner?

One only has to take a closer look at those around and evidence of leadership is everywhere. Believing in the possibilities of others is a foundation of growth. For we inherently have traits that differentiate us. These traits evolve with guidance. I encourage you to expect the best from people. Encourage their efforts and mostly to "believe them to success."

That is the game changer formula for leadership success. That is the trademark of an Uncommon Leader.

Chapter One

A

The letter A by itself is just a letter used in the alphabet but when combined with acronyms that inspire action, you have a very different meaning. Here are a few of my favorite leadership behaviors that make a difference for me when interacting with my own managers and peers. A, the first letter…. serving as the "True North" for the rest of the alphabet.

*A*sking relevant questions to get to the heart of the matter.

*A*ssume not, as we all know where that leads.

*A*ccuracy enables a solid account of what is being assessed or decided. Conclusions are drawn from the buildup of facts. Think about how many times you have come to a decision where if you had just asked a question or two, your decision would have been very different. One of the most important steps in the mental cycle is knowing the difference between your pre-judgement based on someone's interpretation and factual conclusion. While this is not rocket science, it is one of the hardest things for a common leader to remember. It requires practice and discipline on a daily basis.

*A*ctions are set based on mutually-derived conclusions. Once a good understanding is established, then the end result is one that is of common agreement. With this in mind, clear actions and follow-ups are discussed and the forward strategy is put in play.

Chapter Two
B

While B is the second letter in the alphabet, the leadership association is not any less important than the letter A. In fact, the only way to know the difference is to say your ABCs backwards where B then becomes just as important.

*B*e present, the mindset needed when talking with others. Give intentional and focused attention, and listen sincerely. People know when you are distracted or pretending to listen. Give people quality attention, however short, and they will cherish the connection you make. So, make it a quality session that counts.

*B*are yourself as a person, not a robot so that people can relate to your transparency. Be original and predictable at the same time. Focus on the stated and the unstated. There are areas where people are just not ready to "tell it all." Bear that in mind as you seek to understand the real message.

*B*ase your self-worth on things that matter, like people, not process. Your candor is appreciated in many ways.

One, people need to hear the truth and two, why not tell the truth?

*B*ank the value you add when others respect you as a leader. The payoff is priceless and fulfilling, especially in those moments of leadership loneliness.

Chapter Three

C

At the core of the human spirit is the desire to develop a meaningful pathway in life. The "Core" or "Center" is the defining point of where one is. Depending on where you are in life the letter "C" serves as the "Center" of one's life; The beginning, the middle or the end. And to the uncommon leader, "C" is the "Clarity" of words, thoughts and actions serving as the "Center."

---

*C*larity finds its way to you once all the right questions are asked, and examples are shared. In the absence of clarity, uncommon leaders formulate judgement based on facts, knowing that premature judgement can cause havoc on someone's character.

*C*haracter establishes whether one is genuine or not. It helps answer the question: "do they really care about me?" or "are they just acting like they do?" Uncommon leaders ensure this is answered definitively.

*C*reative support for people who have "bright ideas." Never leaving talent uncovered. This is simply "believing people to success."

*C*ustomize the foundation for each person based on their abilities and desire to succeed. People are all different in one way or another, so treat them that way. Differences are not always flawless, they are just differences, so keep your assessment of flaws intact.

*C*ontracts are not always in writing. Some are person to person, eye to eye, or even an old fashion hand shake. Partake in ways that show you are human, not all dotted lines are "dotted."

Chapter Four

D

Deepening the knowledge, you have of others is not only the right way of understanding who is on your team, but it also shows how you want to learn and apply the knowledge you gain about them.

---

*D*istinguish yourself by caring about others. It is rare in these times of instant gratification.

*D*etermine why you do what you do and state your purpose - this way the real meaning is displayed. You will quickly see how this allows for varying degrees of action.

*D*isengage yourself from external distractions which sometimes take you off course - it's the last place you want to be - distractions can be "energy vampires."

*D*epend on others for support, it is inclusive and shows a welcoming vulnerability. Leadership is not a one-way path. No one enjoys a "Team of One," It takes more than one to make a team.

*D*ig deep to really create the swift action required to move people forward. Identify their hidden potentials and possibilities and let them soar by the promise of your support.

Chapter Five

E

Excellence, Engaging, and Executive are all familiar terms in the corporate world and even in religious places of worship. Who are we worshiping? God is everywhere so why do we go to places that don't require us to go? This is not a book to preach to you but why not if the people we worship are not even people, they are titles.

---

*E*arn your stripes through the work it takes to succeed, no shortcuts, no cheating. In short, don't expect special favors. Work smart, hard, and show your flexibility through true actions and results, not words and graphs that are subject to interpretation.

*E*verybody counts! You may get to decide who gets promoted or gets a raise. However, those choices create a problem when results are not delivered in accordance with the reward. Ensure you evaluate performance fairly and without bias. Guess who the "Executive" looks at then? Yes, You.

*E*vergreen is not just a color in the Crayola box, it is also a way of managing your team. A pure form of delivery from your heart. Capitalize on every opportunity to show leadership. Your own and theirs.

Chapter Six
F

From time to time we keep asking ourselves why we do what we do. It's really not a surprise that we are interested in people that make a difference. Here are a few things to consider when it's your turn to do just that.

*F*reedom from worry that what they do will matter. Uncommon leaders ensure they validate the worth of others - they ensure the team knows they matter. It's your role as a leader to bring that into fruition.

*F*reelance, allowing your team to come full circle. The way you start off with them is how you will end with them. Circles are perfectly rounded, a key trait of leaders that are considered uncommon. Perfection may be the ultimate destination, remember your team is human - allow them to develop their unique skills.

*F*ear as a tool marks the insecurity of a poor leader. If you have ever tried it, your testimony will show you ended up right where you started. The blame game only works a few times before the source is traced back to the leader. So, change your strategy.

*F*ace the reality of situations as they arise. The truth in the moment drives confidence and results. Uncommon leaders lead forward with determination and truth. That delivers the desired results.

*F*ocus is a necessary ingredient when delivering a message. Seeking understanding falls in the same sphere too. Ever delivered a message that left people wondering? Ever delivered messages that missed the mark? Give people hope by conveying messages with care and candor and they will apply with confidence and return for reinforcement.

Chapter Seven

G

In many companies there are people who come and go. Which one do you want to be? The one that comes or the one that goes? Keep reading to see where you end up.

---

*G*angster Boss is one way to get there, but we all know where gangsters end up. I don't know about you but that is a different way of going off the grid. Ok back to the best ways to lead and that includes some humor. LOL

*G*ratitude is an excellent way to show people that what they do for you as their leader is appreciated. Taking people for granted is the fastest way to dwindle down your numbers; All of them.

*G*reatness requires ongoing attempts to get it right. Quitting is not an option even if failing is a way to learn, which most of the time, it is.

Come back and see where you are now. Have you decided if you're coming or going? Keep moving forward because it is the only way to succeed.

Chapter Eight

H

Have you ever heard of a double-edged sword? It's a weapon that has two edges, both will injure you if someone were to yank it from you. It's a weapon you would handle with great care to avoid hurting yourself. Hearing someone out works the same way. Why the comparison? Because it's not very different when you hurt someone's feelings. The pain can be harsh when someone you look up to is hurting people with their words. Just because there is no blade, does not mean you're not "cutting" them.

---

*H*earing from the heart is plain and simple. Put yourself in their shoes so you don't stub someone's toe. Meaning, don't forget where you came from as the shoe was on your foot at one point.

*H*andle emotions with care. If you observe that someone is having a hard time, telling them to go figure it out is really not helping, now it is? It may be getting them out of your office for the moment but they will be back. Help people solve their problems by listening and providing actionable guidance.

*H*elping your team will always work in your favor. A non-judging ear can help in more ways than you think. Allow them to think and process. You can guide the conversation as genuine concerns are shared. Genuine concerns result in genuine solutions that last, making a real difference.

Chapter Nine

I

I, I, and I, as you can see there is no one person who you can say it better or worse than you, when there is only you. Now how is a team supposed to be a team when it's only you looking in the mirror and saying, "I am running the show." You're not running the show, you're running away from reality. Forget the I and go for the team approach. Here is how.

---

*I*ndependence can be a wonderful thing when all there is, is you. Leaders lead others, so your vision of independence is really over while you are at work. Actually, it's not different at home either. You more than likely have a family that you help lead every day. Keep that thought when you are in the office too.

*I*ntegration is essential when working with your team. Meetings are great and you can cover a lot, however, encourage your team to also work together when you are not around. How many times have you said nothing in a meeting and as soon as the "boss" leaves, you are all talk? Same concept. Feel free to leave the room.

*I*nquire, ask the hard questions that must be asked, be the one to speak up. Show your team how to do that. Have them take your place in a meeting and expect them to ask and practice this skill in real time.

*I*t's like everything else you learn, if you do not put the skills into practice it will wither up on the shelf. Create the opportunities for them.

Chapter Ten
J

Jumping for joy! When you see results, this is what you do. It's not a question of should I or does that really matter, it's more a question of, how do I show them how good a job they are doing as a team. And how they contribute to the bottom line. Nobody should lose sight of this, so all these proven traits are for your benefit too. When your numbers are solid and real, truly moving in the right direction, you will have the validation of "Team Work"

---

*J*ustification has many meanings but one that is key, is keeping your word. It justifies that what you are doing as a team leader is working and that they get credit for their contribution. How many times did you do all the work and your name was mentioned nowhere? How did that make you feel? I know you received a paycheck for it, but did that really motivate you to keep going at that speed or step on your own to volunteer to work on a project? My guess is no. Do your part and show how they did theirs. Omitting this, will have you working alone so fast, leaving your head spinning.

*J*ubilee is another way of showing how togetherness is working for the greater good. It represents happy people and if people can be happy at work, it's a major contributor to happy homes.

*J*ust be you - reflecting when you were in their position and always kept joy as a target. Celebrate and elevate your team for recognition in ways that resonate with them. If you are unsure what they like, ask them.

Chapter Eleven

K

Let's spell "Kandy" with a K instead of a C. Does that make the candy less sweet because it's spelled differently? No, in fact, it attracts more attention and piques curious interest to try out that new "Kandy" instead of the Candy. So, be the storefront that prepares the "Kandy" over the normal Candy. Here is how.

---

*K*eeping your eye out for talent is a key attribute of a leader. Attract different skilled individuals and mold their talent to their benefit.

*K*indle with people who want to learn as leaders thrive on teaching and learning constantly.

*K*assandra, we will say, will also want what you have and you will always want to give it to her.

*K*eepers of mental health is basically a way of saying; they care about what you think.

*K*nowledge gained is knowledge shared at any given point. It's the way leaders think, always preparing for their replacement. A very unselfish way of thinking about how to be an effective manager and leader. The two are not the same. A manager is one who oversees people and the work they do. A leader shows them the best way to do the work and create self-reliance.

Do you know that your team can identify if you are effective or not? I am a firm believer that every person adds value in one way or another, and so who are we as leaders to keep them in a box with boundaries? Why characterize them as "worker b's" vs "leader a's." Just know that you have the ability to bring out the best in each person.

Chapter Twelve

L

Leaning forward will always keep you ahead of the game. Afterall, who wants to "restrain" someone in a place they do not want to be. This really means that if you keep your team stable, that is good but , don't leaders want greatness from people? The difference truly is changing someone's way of life through heightened and intentional expectations and experiences

---

*L*eading people is not just a workplace anthem. It's a conversation that happens at work but not always about work. Leaders care not only about your happiness at work but also your homelife. Why? Because we know that one impacts the other, so, the real question is, why not?

*L*ingerers are people who stick around for the paycheck. As they should, I mean you do work to get paid, but what if your paychecks came with a person who cared about you? Leaders do just that. They care about you enough to spend their time developing you into the next opportunity and helping you realize your vision.

*L*ove what you're doing or do something else. If you are not coming to your place of work or anywhere for that matter from a place of "loving what you are doing," I urge you to do something else. Why waste people's time with insincerity? If you don't care, they won't either.

Perfect people do not exist, but authentic leaders do try to be the best people leaders they can be. A well-rounded person is more effective and influential than a self-centered individual.

Chapter Thirteen

M

Mastery is not what you think it is, meaning it has nothing to do with control. It's actually the opposite. Giving up control is way more important than gaining control or keeping control as you will soon find out. The only thing you control is your own actions. Not that of anyone else.

---

*M*ind your manners when talking with others, show you have some" home training". You know, "please" and "thank you?" You know, common sense stuff? Well, we heard common sense isn't common, anyway, be mindful of your approach.

*M*ild-mannered has a strength of its own - this skill is unthreatening while showing you care. Coupled with great follow up, your team will understand that you appreciate them. If you observe them having a bad day, or even bad moments, offer help. Uncover the issues and master managing emotions including your own.

*M*undane is a perfect way to show someone to the door before quitting time. When someone's routine is so mundane, you're basically saying, "you're done here," before they even got started. Stop making people feel like they are just going through the motions. All you will get from them is motion. No results! No commitment! Show support.

Mothers will always say, they are caring and helpful, but if you make them mad enough, you will see another not so attractive side. Be the" mother" that makes your team feel like they "belong." Deliver the "tough love" wrapped in caring.

Moving on down the road as we continue to read about how common people need uncommon leaders.

Chapter Fourteen

N

Newbies may not necessarily be new to the organization; many a times, they are new to their roles as a result of internal promotions. Keeping that in mind when interacting is important as their contributions more than likely played a role in their promotion. Design a different leadership position that leverages their experience to help the overall team goals. It's a great way to show you appreciate their addition to your team and shows them they matter right off the bat.

*N*aysayers are people who say, "No" to just about everything. No aspiring leader needs the distraction nor do established leaders. By creating a progressive anthem of, "let's get it done" any circle of leaders assures that the team will work through challenges and surmount barriers as they arise.

"*N*o problem, that idea is great, do the research, get the facts and then let's see if it makes sense". This should be your "go to" phrase. Practice it!

"*N*ever come to me with a problem, only solutions." How many times has one of your managers told that to their team? I lost count honestly. That's such an oxymoron quote. How on earth does someone come up with solutions when nobody understands the problem in the first place? Discuss the problem, PLEASE. Tenacity to tackle a problem requires you to discuss it and not assume your team knows what the heck you're talking about. They don't! Thank you.

Unfulfilled dreams are only unfulfilled ways of doing nothing. So, do something that helps fulfill dreams not fill them up with despair.

Chapter Fifteen
O

Ordinary is as boring as someone who has watched the same movie over and over again. Can you put in a new movie for them? Can you be the movie director of a new movie for others? Can you put on the uniform of the guy who makes the popcorn and take the tickets at the counter so clients can get in? If you can't, this book is not for you. You will need a book about how to be a manager. This book is about how to be a leader and for years, I served popcorn to not just my team but many other teams too. This was a new event we added to our calendars just to show our teams that we would do whatever it took to support them.

---

*O*range is a color of many fruits and veggies. But it's not a color of time. Be prepared to give more than 100% of your time. I know that's not physically possible but it may feel that way some days.

*O*rganize what you are working on in order of importance so nothing falls through the cracks. Some cracks go all the way to the button of the earth and since we are not all geologists, we cannot tell the extent of these "cracks".

*O*riginate new opportunities for people so they can have options. Make a way for others to see that you are creative in your style. Everyone has creativity within - encourage a collaborative environment that brings the best of people to the surface.

*O*thers will come to you and ask, "how did you get your quality so high?" Your best position is giving credit to the team for getting things done. Afterall, they did it, right?

Chapter Sixteen

P

Personality is the outward projection of our inward emotions. Allow your team and those around you to project the plethora of emotions that is stirring within themselves - in a safe and supportive environment.

*P*eople with a capital P is the core of who leaders are. There is no question about it. All that needs to be said about the matter is captured in the sentence above.

*P*erson to person is a preferred method, however, that does not stop a leader by any means. A leader will figure out what works for the majority and make it happen. Never does a leader allow excuses to stand in the way of progress. It just does not happen. This mentality does not exist. I am not sure if that is a skill taught or if that is what is meant by "A natural born leader" but it's a close match.

*P*ersonality should always be good or as good as you can make it. It is an added plus. There is no reason for someone in a leadership position to have a bad attitude. Leaders may have bad moments, not extended bad attitudes.

*P*rivacy is not just a personal preference; it is very much a vital necessity in the workplace. If this sounds a lot like trust, it is. It is the difference between employees confidently sharing information, and suffering in silence. Privacy means you care enough to respect privacy. Your opportunity to do this ceases with a breach of trust. Leaders must protect their reputation.

*P*erfection is an aspirational goal and is accompanied by a steep price tag. Leaders strive for perfection and land on excellence. Leaders should always be willing to pay the price for excellence.

*P*rovide the voice of reason when things feel completely unreasonable. Chaos quickly steers an orderly team off course. Create balance by leveraging the strengths of your team and know when to throw down the anchors so no one goes overboard and drowns in their own misstep. It's your duty to keep the ship afloat.

Chapter Seventeen

Q

In the quiet stillness of the moment, the soul finds solace and direction to plow on. Establishing the cadence and rhythm of success.

---

*Q*uitters throw the towel in, denying themselves the opportunity to see things to the end. The decision to quit is the blind act to "go it alone." I am not sure when someone decides to quit if they just say to themself, "I am done" or if they just do that momentarily. Either way when things get to what seems like a point of no return, leaders will make it a point to intervene: stray from the current path and chart a new course to make the process easier. They find ways to make things work.

*Q*uiet time is so important not just for yourself but for everyone else too. Anytime you desire to "micro-watch" someone closely, that is a clear indication of going too far. Leaders know when to back up and give space, and when to offer progressive support. In short - leaders give their teams the space to "breathe."

Quenching what is known as "career hunger" is paramount to progress. Leaders know this empowering action is a significant action to a team. Keep your team challenged and grow promotable people through developmental activities such as coaching and mentorship. You just might enjoy it too.

Come on down the aisle and see what lies behind door number 1. I guarantee the anomaly will prove to be worthy of your time.

Chapter Eighteen

R

Realization is a moment of understanding why we do what we do. Why we care. Who taught us to be this person? If you're anything like me, it's not how we do something, it's why we do it. Leaders have to come to individual conclusions. In the interest of sharing what I discovered, it's important to understand why people seek out certain leaders. If you are a sought-out leader, you must be intentional with your actions. This is the reality of being a leader of people. That is the responsibility.

*R*eally? is not just a way of asking is that right? It's an echo affirming why you're here. Your reality. You're not asking if you're really here, because you are. In the off chance that you are asking about your reality, Then it's really real. Are you wondering what I am talking about yet? Good. Keep reading...

*R*ealization keeps you focused and will get you to your goal, no matter what. Real things are kept real if you focus on them. They only fall off the board, if you let your ideas, we will say, sit unattended with no focus or life-giving actions toward making them real. Restrictions keep you sitting around and trying to figure out where to go next, but realization does the opposite. It nurtures ideas and gives birth possibilities. Clear Yet? Keep going…

Rays of sun make things grow: people, plants and trees. Add water to sun rays and magic happens. Consider yourself the sun and the water for the production of ideas and concepts. You can make good ideas live or die by watering them with leadership nuggets or let them wither by development deprivation. Don't ever think you can't make a difference, you can.

Reveal what you have uncovered in your team. Expose, promote and lift them up to the higher-ups, like you would do if you found a precious diamond among black stones. Your voice carries weight to the next level, so the more the life you create, the stronger your leadership muscles grow.

Chapter Nineteen

S

What would the world be like without the sounds of silence? How would we function if we did not experience the break in silence with laughter and song? How enriching each is, uniquely complementing each other.

*S*olid foundation lasts longer than shaky ground. Where would you rather stand, on solid rock or a shaky ground? Now I am for adventure but when it comes to my paycheck and where I spend most of my time, I am going for the biggest immovable rock I can find. Guess where leaders fall in the puzzle? Yep, you're the rock.

*S*ounds of laughter are just as important as the sounds of the keyboard strokes clicking away. One without the other is very one sided.

*S*angria got its name because its color is dark red like blood. This is not turning into a fiction novel or anything such thing. But I do want to show how important it is to have skin in the game. To form a bond of "uni-purpose" that is held together by trust, integrity and aligned goals. Set goals with your team as stakeholders and watch them work to exceed. No real person wants to be told what to do and not knowing without understanding the whys. Inclusion or better yet, mass engagement is still the best answer to plan your team's path to success. Someone smart chose red for Sangria.

Chapter Twenty

T

Teachers are the heart and soul of educational experiences. Do you remember your first teacher? I remember mine; Ma Sarah in a rural school who was my second adult teaching me how to work with others. Her lessons of doing the right thing, still echoes in my being. That's the effect of uncommon leaders, leaving echoes of conscience to the listener.

---

*T*ender actions do not require a tender face per say. Firm and gentle do co-exist. Be yourself by all means, but be the best version of yourself. The relatable, likeable leader.

*T*enacious is a strong word and inspires hard work. Tenacity is the skill that gets you going in that direction. Help the ones you lead arrive to experience tasks of all size and scope and guide them to actualization. Think "Stretch to win."

*T*actful is a goodwill currency of providing feedback in a thoughtful and truthful way, without damaging relationships. Tough conversations do not have to be hard. When you are the rock on which they stand, teammates want the stability and guidance through necessary adjustments. So, when adjustments are suggested, leaders must be tactful so change can be embraced.

*T*rying times will lead to jagged edges, a solid rock has the safety net already in place. Keep a Plan B for when some efforts go south. Unexpected jaggedness will be softened with necessary degrees of adjustment - with you in at the helm or leading from behind, the team will hang on, trusting your leadership

Chapter Twenty-One

U

"U" have places to go, people to coach and lessons to teach. U are the leader, there is no one else like U……….. got the message, yet? Read on…….

"*U*nderestimated" is synonymous with "Underappreciated" in the workplace. It's no wonder times are like they are. Where would we be if we overestimated the positive impact of our teams? I mean how often do you think about over preparing our teams as they take the "stage?" There is no question that investing in your team as you invest in yourself is a recipe for compounding success. Prepare your way to the top by preparing your people. You are the most important denominator to your team's success, act like it. In doing so, you will ensure that they are

*U*nwavering in their loyalty. I don't mean loyalty to just the job but to you as the leader.

*U*nderstanding is seeking for the truth and facts to come to a valid conclusion. There is no wrapping this in a pretty, unregulated package. Do the work. Find the untapped potential in both the person and the ideas.

*U*nivision is relevant when seeking the authentic core of
people. A skill many leaders will master with time and
practice. Log your assumptions, and when you collect the
facts, reflect on how far you've come over time. Be the
bridge to progress not the roadblock.

*U*nanimous we stand is a common way leader bring
others together when times get tough. Sharing both blame
and praise. You may think this should say, "United we
stand", but that is different. People can stand around all
day long, but until you're unanimous in why you are
standing rarely does it make a difference. Vision and
agreement count as a core baseline.

Chapter Twenty-Two

V

Victory is the first word that comes to mind, however- it is the last milestone that people acknowledge. Why is that? Is meeting the first milestone as important as the middle and last? Of course, it is. So, make this a priority and you will always come in first place.

---

*V*alidate when someone comes to talk with you. This means acknowledging them by name, and getting to know what matters most to them. Making a personal connection validates the essence of who they are. At a minimum, help them create a path by showing them the ropes of the place.

*V*aledictorian is a great title signifying the echelon of high school accomplishment. What then is the equivalent in the workplace? Teams have missions and goals. People have passion and aspirations. Create corporate valedictorians by recognizing the value in your team. The goals, mission, and plans are all essential to achieving the "corporate valedictorian" status.

*V*elocity is a key driver at the center of what people work to achieve. The more they like what they are working on, the better the results. Move your team around and allow them to have input on what they work on. Permitting your team to experience multiple roles, accelerates the results and creates synergy. Create momentum, encourage gentle velocity to enhance sustainable growth.

Chapter Twenty-Three

W

Wonder why we want what we want? That's a lot of "w's" What wonderful effects "W" has on people. "W" is associated with "The Win, The Wow Factor," The Wonderful and the best of the best." I look at this as two VVs not one letter W. If you can guess why, you're on your way to a very successful leadership experience. Still wondering? Keep reading.

---

*W*hy would you ever come to work and think you are a winner all by yourself? It's another way of saying, I am in this alone and the work of others did not contribute to the success of the company. This is how a solo attitude is interpreted. How long do you think your self-absorption would be tolerated? Respect for the contributions of others is what makes a team work.

*W*ishful-thinking can drive you crazy when all you want is someone to step up and be a leader. It takes a leader to create a leader. You will encounter people with very good work ethics and "can do attitudes," however, until you take those people under your wing and model leadership traits for them, they will forever be stuck. Be a game changer, Bring others along.

Keep wondering, keep seeking and keep going until you see what you need to see when you need to see it. There is talent everywhere but it's up to you to bring it to the surface.

Chapter Twenty-Four
X

Obviously, X-Ray is going to be on this page but not for the reasons you may think. When you think of an X-Ray, I am sure you compare that to visiting the doctor's office, wearing a gown, taking a "picture" of your anatomy and then giving you the news. Well, this is a little different. This is more about excellence in the workplace. See below for more details

---

"*X*" marks the spot when you are a leader in the workplace, by this I mean you are the X-Man and everyone else can be superheroes too. There is a leader and a team of top performers that all defeat the enemy or in this case, accomplish the mission given down from the spaceship, (Let's call them Head Honchos). This is what a good X-Ray looks like in the workplace. Now the reason I used X-Ray as the symbol here is because until you see this with as much clarity as an X-ray, you're going to need to keep coming back for another "checkup". Consider it a self-examination. Highly recommended on a regular basis no matter what. Keep re-examining yourself for touch ups and growth of good tissues.

XXX can be a trilogy of many things, 3 strikes you are out, 3 X 1 = 3, but no matter how you look at it, it's still more than one. That is the whole point of a leader. Not how many people you lead, but how many are you showing how to lead. Aim high and no matter how many times you come up to bat, you will always have a winning record. Share your tips until you're all tipped out. All knowledge is fair game. Share the playbook so everyone is playing by the same rules.

Chapter Twenty-Five

Y

You are worthy of achieving your dreams. You are endowed with the foundation to get it done, you owe it to yourself to transfer that to others so that the circle of success continues to infinity, and that is the mission and that is the leadership promise.

---

*Y*ellow is one of the brightest colors; but there is always a way to get brighter. Keep from tanning yourself with lotions and use the real sunshine, nature's portion. Obviously, a metaphor for keeping yourself at peace and not pretending you're at peace. Nothing shows more in a leader than when your "real" suntan is fake. Be Real!

*Y*et again when there are others who tell you one thing and do another, it stimulates the questions that may or may not get asked. Example: "Is this guy for real? what's in it for him?' If your team is going to follow up in a way that is loyal, let your actions speak louder than your words. This will keep the "hush-talk" to a non-factual basis for people who want to do something else with their lives.

*Y*ielding when the light is yellow is what we are all taught in driving class, but yielding in the middle of top-notch initiative is a sure way to crash. Pick up momentum when you see things shifting to the yielding zone. Allow another to take the wheel when a teammate needs a pause. Help them understand no one is tracking them so closely to create a fear of failure. Promote doing what's right for the team. No one is going to blindside them if your communication is as open as it should be.

Chapter Twenty-Six
Z

Zion is a place in the Bible where Jesus was born and is called his place or home. Where is your home? Is it in the office? At happy hour with coworkers? Keep asking yourself the question until you find the answer. If you have more than one answer. Good luck keeping up the momentum. People need an escape from work, so when they are home, leave them alone and let them be at home. If you have not been invited for dinner, why are you talking to them at dinner time? Is there something so important that it can't wait until the next business day? If you say yes to this question, keep asking yourself where your home is?

Zinc is a common vital element that keeps your body from growing more things than it should. Everyone likes growth in the company numbers but no one likes growths that are disposable. If you keep growing people to be workaholics, you are unknowingly creating negative growth. Know what the probable outcome will be? Yes, employees avoiding you like the plague. I am not going to preach work-life balance but I am going to preach to work and live in separate places. In your mind at least.

Zeal rhymes with peel and the only reference to rhymes in the chapter is to make sure you rhyme with someone who has an unmistakable presence, energy creation, expendable and shareable energy for the good. It's ok to watch from the sidelines but don't be silent.

As we have reached the end of the ABC's of Leadership, it certainly does not end here. Take each one of these pages and create a journal of your own growth and those of others. How else will you know how far you've come. One day you will validate your own impact by the notes you have written and the testimonies of those you have helped establish as leaders in the world on their own terms.

Chapter 28
The ABC's of the Inner You

Once the alphabet ends, I am sure you thought the book would end but it does not. In fact, it's just the beginning. I am not going to repeat each letter for this section but I am going to keep you focused on A, B, and C.

A is a way of judging the kind of person you are. It really stands as the top of anything. For purposes of this section we are going to call it "Body Type." Having an "A" body type is a very significant rating. Just like you would see in a Standard and Poor's rating. Triple A ratings are very secure, reliable and can be trusted to work with. This is where you should aim to be. Aim to be the very best person you can be both in your mind, heart and spirit. Not only is this the winning combination, it's the easiest, best version of your life. Spend your life here not where the ratings are risky and could go up or down at any time.

B will keep you going with great stride. B = "Spirit Type." Don't worry this will not turn into a spiritual book unless you want it to be. And this is really the point. Do you want your life to be a "going through the motions" life? or one that is led by the Christ that lives inside of you. I'll let you in on a little secret; Keeping yourself at bay without GOD is what happens when you focus on your mind and not your heart as part of the combination for success.   Try this as a best practice and that is where you will end up. A Triple A.

C is just that, it's your conscious. The way you really feel about things and people lie in the depths of your inner self. Come out of that place with all you have, come clean from the things you're not proud of and let them be forgiven by Christ in you. Once that is done there is only good awaiting you.

Peace be with you.

Acknowledgement

To 8 extraordinary leaders who allowed a 'Little Girl from Africa" to steer the helm of a ship of creative excellence. And a phenomenal Coach, Tommie Y. English, who believed her "Bull" could fly.

About the Author

Effua McGowan, Founder of Amazing You, LLC. An organization dedicated to the development of global human capital. She has over 24 years of senior corporate experience, including serving as a Vice President at JP Morgan Chase, leading multimillion-dollar businesses across the USA. Effua collaborates with universities and organizations globally, including the USA and several African countries.

Educated in Liberia, Kenya, Swaziland, The Ivory Coast, The United States including emerging programs in France, Effua is a multi-lingual expert in advancing the human capacity of organizations, helping them strategically align their talent to preserve their competitive edge. She holds a Masters of Management in Human Resource Management.

Effua designs and facilitates leadership and diversity programs for corporate and community clients. Her leadership programs and workshops have been adapted and applied globally. She has designed and facilitated development programs for diverse groups and is recognized globally winning her numerous awards.

Married to Harold McGowan for 33 years, and a mother of three amazing young adults (in my heart), to whom she has introduced the love of diversity. In her spare time, Effua loves to read, travel and enjoys the company of family, friends and meeting new acquaintances.

Effua is donating 100% of proceeds to benefit the establishment of a new elementary/early childhood school in rural Liberia and the promotion of mental health and wellness in the country.